SandCastle 3

Long Vowels

Uū

Mary Elizabeth Salzmann

ABDO
Publishing Company

Published by SandCastle™, an imprint of ABDO Publishing Company, 4940 Viking Drive, Edina, Minnesota 55435.

Printed in the United States.

Cover and Interior Photo credits: Artville, Comstock, Corbis Images, Digital Vision, Photodisc

Library of Congress Cataloging-in-Publication Data

Salzmann, Mary Elizabeth, 1968-
    Uu / Mary Elizabeth Salzmann.
        p. cm. -- (Long vowels)
    Includes index.
    ISBN 1-57765-417-X
    [1. English language--Phonetics.] I. Title.

PE1119 .S23425 2000
428.1--dc21
                                                                    00-033212

The SandCastle concept, content, and reading method have been reviewed and approved by a national advisory board including literacy specialists, librarians, elementary school teachers, early childhood education professionals, and parents.

Let Us Know

After reading the book, SandCastle would like you to tell us your stories about reading. What is your favorite page? Was there something hard that you needed help with? Share the ups and downs of learning to read. We want to hear from you! To get posted on the Abdo Publishing Company Web site, send us email at:

sandcastle@abdopub.com

About SandCastle™
Nonfiction books for the beginning reader

- Basic concepts of phonics are incorporated with integrated language methods of reading instruction. Most words are short, and phrases, letter sounds, and word sounds are repeated.

- Readability is determined by the number of words in each sentence, the number of characters in each word, and word lists based on curriculum frameworks.

- Full-color photography reinforces word meanings and concepts.

- "Words I Can Read" list at the end of each book teaches basic elements of grammar, helps the reader recognize the words in the text, and builds vocabulary.

- Reading levels are indicated by the number of flags on the castle.

Look for more SandCastle books
in these three reading levels:

Level 1 (one flag)	**Level 2** (two flags)	**Level 3** (three flags)

Grades Pre-K to K 5 or fewer words per page	**Grades K to 1** 5 to 10 words per page	**Grades 1 to 2** 10 to 15 words per page

Here are fun ways to truly
have a super day.

Uberto and Judy have
fun learning to use the
computer.

Udele and Julie wear tutus
and crowns for their play.

Ula uses three inner tubes to have fun at Malibu Beach.

Uū

Uma likes to spin her super hula hoop around her hips.

Umar has a mule named Ruby.

He gives Ruby a huge hug.

Uri and Ruth look very
cute in their new costumes.

We play music in our white and orange band uniforms.

19

Ushi likes to practice tunes outside.

What instrument is she playing?

(flute)

Words I Can Read

Nouns

A noun is a person, place, or thing

computer (kuhm-PYOO-tur) p. 7
costumes (KOSS-toomz) p. 17
crowns (KROUNZ) p. 9
day (DAY) p. 5
flute (FLOOT) p. 21
fun (FUHN) pp. 7, 11

hips (HIPSS) p. 13
hug (HUHG) p. 15
hula hoop (HOO-luh hoop) p. 13
inner tubes (IN-ur toobz) p. 11
instrument (IN-struh-muhnt) p. 21

mule (MYOOL) p. 15
music (MYOO-zik) p. 19
play (PLAY) p. 9
tunes (TOONZ) p. 21
tutus (TOO-tooz) p. 9
uniforms (YOO-nuh-formz) p. 19
ways (WAYZ) p. 5

Proper Nouns

A proper noun is the name of a person, place, or thing

Judy (JOO-dee) p. 7
Julie (JOO-lee) p. 9
Malibu Beach (MAL-i-boo BEECH) p. 11
Ruby (ROO-bee) p. 15

Ruth (ROOTH) p. 17
Uberto (OO-bair-toh) p. 7
Udele (OO-del) p. 9
Ula (OO-luh) p. 11

Uma (OO-muh) p. 13
Umar (OO-mar) p. 15
Uri (OOR-ee) p. 17
Ushi (OO-shee) p. 21

Pronouns

A pronoun is a word that replaces a noun

he (HEE) p. 15
she (SHEE) p. 21

we (WEE) p. 19

what (WUHT) p. 21

22

Verbs

A verb is an action or being word

are (AR) p. 5
flute (FLOOT) p. 21
gives (GIVZ) p. 15
has (HAZ) p. 15
have (HAV) pp. 5, 7, 11
is (IZ) p. 21

learning (LURN-ing) p. 7
likes (LIKESS) pp. 13, 21
look (BUK) p. 17
named (NAYMD) p. 15
play (PLAY) p. 19
playing (PLAY-ing) p. 21

practice (PRAK-tiss) p. 21
spin (SPIN) p. 13
use (YOOZ) p. 7
uses (YOOZ-ez) p. 11
wear (WAIR) p. 9

Adjectives

An adjective describes something

band (BAND) p. 19
cute (KYOOT) p. 17
fun (FUHN) p. 5
her (HUR) p. 13

huge (HYOOJ) p. 15
new (NOO) p. 17
orange (OR-inj) p. 19
our (AR) p. 19

super (SOO-pur) pp. 5, 13
their (THAIR) pp. 9, 17
three (THREE) p. 11
white (WITE) p. 19

Adverbs

An adverb tells how, when, or where something happens

here (HIHR) p. 5

outside (out-SIDE) p. 21

truly (TROO-lee) p. 5
very (VER-ee) p. 17

23

Glossary

computer – a machine that can store, process, and retrieve information.

hula hoop – a plastic hoop that is twirled around the body.

instrument – a device used to make music.

uniform – special clothes worn by all members of a group.

More Uū Words

bugle	graduate	rude
community	June	rule
cube	July	truth
duty	lunar	tulip
emu	monument	useful
fuse	produce	yule